Kenneth Born

Did Basel III miss the point?

The role of IFRS's Other Comprehensive Income during the financial crisis

Anchor Academic Publishing

Born, Kenneth: Did Basel III miss the point? The role of IFRS's Other Comprehensive Income during the financial crisis, Hamburg, Anchor Academic Publishing 2017

Buch-ISBN: 978-3-96067-105-3
PDF-eBook-ISBN: 978-3-96067-605-8
Druck/Herstellung: Anchor Academic Publishing, Hamburg, 2017
Covermotiv: © pixabay.de

Bibliografische Information der Deutschen Nationalbibliothek:
Die Deutsche Nationalbibliothek verzeichnet diese Publikation in der Deutschen Nationalbibliografie; detaillierte bibliografische Daten sind im Internet über http://dnb.d-nb.de abrufbar.

Bibliographical Information of the German National Library:
The German National Library lists this publication in the German National Bibliography. Detailed bibliographic data can be found at: http://dnb.d-nb.de

All rights reserved. This publication may not be reproduced, stored in a retrieval system or transmitted, in any form or by any means, electronic, mechanical, photocopying, recording or otherwise, without the prior permission of the publishers.

Das Werk einschließlich aller seiner Teile ist urheberrechtlich geschützt. Jede Verwertung außerhalb der Grenzen des Urheberrechtsgesetzes ist ohne Zustimmung des Verlages unzulässig und strafbar. Dies gilt insbesondere für Vervielfältigungen, Übersetzungen, Mikroverfilmungen und die Einspeicherung und Bearbeitung in elektronischen Systemen.

Die Wiedergabe von Gebrauchsnamen, Handelsnamen, Warenbezeichnungen usw. in diesem Werk berechtigt auch ohne besondere Kennzeichnung nicht zu der Annahme, dass solche Namen im Sinne der Warenzeichen- und Markenschutz-Gesetzgebung als frei zu betrachten wären und daher von jedermann benutzt werden dürften.

Die Informationen in diesem Werk wurden mit Sorgfalt erarbeitet. Dennoch können Fehler nicht vollständig ausgeschlossen werden und die Diplomica Verlag GmbH, die Autoren oder Übersetzer übernehmen keine juristische Verantwortung oder irgendeine Haftung für evtl. verbliebene fehlerhafte Angaben und deren Folgen.

Alle Rechte vorbehalten

© Anchor Academic Publishing, Imprint der Diplomica Verlag GmbH
Hermannstal 119k, 22119 Hamburg
http://www.diplomica-verlag.de, Hamburg 2017
Printed in Germany

ABSTRACT

The broad consensus before the recent financial crisis was that the so called fair value accounting (FVA) improves transparency contrary to the historical cost model.[1] Since 2008, the discussion has been on the root cause of the crisis, which lessons can be gleaned from it and how to avoid the same mistakes. Basel III was implemented in order to improve the regulatory environment and was the response of regulators and politicians to public pressure and suspicions raised by the bail out programmes for banks. Consequently, an until then inconceivable number of new regulations and regulatory bodies were introduced.

FVA was also blamed as part of the cause of the recent financial crisis.[2] Available-for Sales (AfS) securities represent a major component of bank balance sheet asset. Gains and losses of AfS-positions are recorded within the Other Comprehensive Income (OCI). The OCI includes items which are not recognized (IAS 1.7) in income statements but increase or decrease a bank's equity. The items also include income and expenses from Available-for Sales positions (AfS) in accordance with IAS 39.

On October 13th 2008, an amendment to IAS 39 was published by IASB. This amendment did authorize the reclassification of assets. This amendment clearly demonstrates the influence of FVA on the value of assets of banks that apply IFRS. The main objective of this book is to verify the influence of 'Other Comprehensive Income' and whether the new regulations sufficiently capture this critical factor (for example, in terms of prudential filters).

Regulators should ensure that unrealized profits do not result in a capital drain. One way to assure this is to make OCI subject to a prudential filter and to deduct it from regulatory capital, which was the case until CRR became effective on 1 January 2014 (CEBS guideline 2004). Basel III is even less strict than Basel II in that regard. Article 26(1) CRR clearly states that CET1 items must be recognized only in case they are really available to the financial institution for *"unrestricted and immediate use to cover risks or losses as soon as these occur"*. Nevertheless, with the introduction of the CRR, the prudential filter for positions that caused the financial crisis and led to poor capitalization of banks was not strengthened but actually removed. At present, CRR does not envisage any filter for unrealized gains parked in Other Comprehensive Income.

---

[1] Casabona / Shoaf, 2010. P.5.
[2] Kholmy, 2012. P.22.

TABLE OF CONTENTS

Abstract 1

Table of Figures 4

List of Abbreviations 5

1 Context of the debate and Approach 7

    1.1 Research questions 10

        1.1.1 Does the concept of OCI allow capital to leave the bank, although gains have not yet been realized? 10

        1.1.2 Is the poor capitalization of several banks also a result of the IFRS's OCI concept? ... 10

        1.1.3 Has the problem been properly addressed by European regulators, in particular in terms of prudential filters? 12

    1.2 Definitions 12

        1.2.1 Financial instruments 12

        1.2.2 Other Comprehensive Income (OCI) 12

        1.2.3 Fair value (FV) 14

        1.2.4 Fair value accounting (FVA) 14

        1.2.5 Financial crisis 14

        1.2.6 Recent financial crisis 14

        1.2.7 Regulatory capital 15

        1.2.8 Regulatory adjustments 16

        1.2.9 Prudential filters 16

        1.2.10 Prudential valuation and prudential filter 16

    1.3 Distribution Policy of Banks 17

    1.4 Overview IAS/IFRS systematic 21

        1.4.1 IAS 39 – Financial instruments: recognition and measurements 21

        1.4.2 IFRS for financial instruments 23

        1.4.3 Fair value accounting – a critical evaluation 23

2 Amendement to IAS 39 and IFRS 7 26
   2.1 What the amendment changed 26
   2.2 Impact of the amendment 30
3 The role of OCI during the recent financial crisis 33
   3.1 OCI and the recent crisis 33
   3.2 The impact on European banks 33
4 Capital requirements and prudential filters 35
   4.1 The removal of prudential filters for unrealized gains and losses recognized in the revaluation reserve – AfS instruments as the largest contributor to changes to Tier 1 capital 35
   4.2 Treatment of AfS positions under the CEBS guideline 2004 35
   4.3 Prudential filters and unrealized gains 36
   4.4 Prudential filters CRR 37
   4.5 Basel III 39
   4.6 Outlook I: EBA Discussion Paper Prudential Filter, 2 August 2013 40
   4.7 RTS on prudent valuation 41
      4.7.1 Consultation paper on RTS on prudent valuation 41
      4.7.2 Final RTS 42
5 Conclusion 44
   5.1 Question 1: Does the concept of OCI allow capital to leave the bank, although profits have not yet been realized? 44
   5.2 Question 2: Is the poor capitalization of several banks also a result of IFRS's concept of OCI? 45
   5.3 Question 3: Has the issue been properly addressed by European regulators, particularly in terms of prudential filters? 45

Bibliography 47

TABLE OF FIGURES

Graph 1: OCI 13
Table 1: Components of regulatory capital 15
Chart 1: Cumulative dividends of 90 European banks since the crisis 18
Chart 2: Frequency distribution of retained earnings by country 2014 19
Chart 3: Annual changes in assets, equity and debt of large European banks 20
Chart 4: IAS 39 Classification of Financial Assets 23
Chart 5: Overview of reclassification options 30
Chart 6: Assets reclassified as a result of amendment to IAS 39 32
Chart 7: Recognizable System Reclassification IAS 39 32
Chart 8: Prudential filters CRR relevant Articles 37
Chart 9: Single Rule Book 2016 4 May: Description of Article 35 CRR 38
Chart 10: Publication of RTS on prudent valuation 42
Chart 11: RTS on prudential valuation 43

LIST OF ABBREVIATIONS

ABS	Asset-Backed Security
AfS	Available for Sale
AVA	Asset Value Adjustment
CDO	Asset-backed Collateralized Debt Obligations
CET1	Common Equity Tier 1
CRR	Capital Requirements Regulation (AVA) Bank for International Settlements (BIS)
EESA	Emergency Economic Stabilization Act
EU	European Union
FASB	Financial Accounting Standards Board
FVA	Fair Value Accounting
HfT	Held for Trading
HtM	Held to Maturity
IAS	International Accounting Standard
IASB	International Accounting Standard Board
IDW	Institut Deutscher Wirtschaftsprüfer
IFRS	International Financial Reporting Standards
LaR	Loans and Receivables
OCI	Other Comprehensive Income
PnL	Profit and Loss
RoA	Return on Assets
RoE	Return on Equity
SEC	Securities Exchange Commission
TARP	Troubled Asset Relief Program

1 CONTEXT OF THE DEBATE AND APPROACH

"…having soundly capitalised banks turns out to be vital for the transmission of monetary policy, also. In this sense, bank capitalisation ought to be a key concern for central banks in fulfilling their monetary policy mandate, as well as for their financial stability mandate…" (Shin Song H. 2016. P.2.)

The regulatory capital of banks, their own funds, is a loss-absorbing buffer. Inadequately capitalized banks may try to improve their solvency by cutting lending. For that reason, it is very often requested to relax bank capital rules. A bank's regulatory capital comes from several sources. The most significant source are retained earnings. The share of own funds represents the accumulated profit stock, that have not been disbursed, for example as dividends to their shareholders.[3]

Since 2007, banks have disbursed significant amounts of cash dividends and bonuses.[4] Regulators are therefore concerned because sufficiently capitalized banks are of upmost importance for the financial stability and therefore for the whole economy. However, interests of different stakeholders, like shareholders and the public, diverge. A complex set of regulations shall make sure, that banks have a sufficient amount of available capital.[5]

The regulatory capital is of course also affected by the assets in banks' balance sheets. Numerous valuation techniques and approaches to value assets exist. There are two extremes in this regard: FVA and the historical cost model.[6]

Before the financial crisis, the broad agreement was that FVA improves transparency in comparison to the historical cost model.[7] The amortized costs approach could not explain the value of a company for a potential investor in a going concern scenario and under market conditions. The assumption was that potential investors were more interested in the fair value,

---

[3] Shin, BIS, 2016. P.1
[4] Shin, BIS, 2016. P.3.
[5] Shin, BIS, 2016. P.3.
[6] Agrimon / Dietsch / Estrada, 2015, P4. „…If unrealised losses are always included, regulatory capital is affected by the inclusion of gains…"
[7] Fiechter, 2011. P. 22.

which denotes the value at which the items can be traded between *"willing and informed"* parties (market prices).[8]

Although FVA certainly has its advantages, market participants around the globe are re-evaluating their practices and regulations. The financial crisis, which began in 2007, exposed the fundamental weaknesses of FVA. In response to the crisis beginning 2007, politicians and regulators introduced an until then inconceivable number of new regulations and new bodies.[9]

In addition to unsustainable banking practices, e.g., delayed loan loss provisions and off-balance sheet financing structures, FVA was also blamed for unleashing the crisis.[10] During and after the crisis, financial institutions suffered immense losses, which had to be written off immediately because of FVA.[11]

The historical cost approach has largely been replaced.[12] FVA is used under IFRS instead. In case there is no active market, banks rely on own models, which base the valuation of an asset on estimated future earnings or cash flows in order to value the FV. This mark-to-model accounting implies discretionary power and consequently, intentional biases.[13]

On 13 October 2008, the International Accounting Standard Board (IASB)[14] issued an amendment to the International Accounting Standard (IAS) 39 authorizing the reclassification of assets. This amendment clearly demonstrates the influence of the FVA on banks' financial statements applying IFRS.[15] Many banks have taken extensive advantage of this new opportunity and have reclassified their assets.

The IASB announced this amendment following a fast procedure and completely avoiding the general due process. Only two days later, the amendment was endorsed[16] and transposed into EU law.[17]

---

[8] Barth, 1994; Shipper, 2005. P.271.
[9] Russo / Katzel, 2011. P.27
[10] Kholmy, 2012. P.1.
[11] Kholmy, 2012. P.3.
[12] Hitz, 2007; Allen and Carletti, 2008. P.323.
[13] Wallison, 2008. P.15
[14] IASB, 2014.
[15] Kholmy, 2012. P.12.
[16] EC Regulation 1004/2008; Kholmy, 2012. P.12.
[17] Ernstberger, 2008. P.16.

Reclassifying banks "avoided substantial fair losses and reported significantly higher regulatory capital" and - for example – also returns on equity.[18]

Politicians and regulators were concerned that FVA plays an important role in the financial crisis.[19] When looking at how Basel III is being implemented, the question arises whether the new regulations actually target the fundamental causes of the financial crisis. In this respect, fair value accounting must be closely scrutinized.

During the financial crisis, the drop in market values – because of illiquid markets- amplified the severity. Financial institutions with significant amounts of financial assets, criticized FVA for its pro-cyclical nature and the resulting losses during a crisis and called for the suspension of FVA approach by putting pressure on politicians to take action.[20] Reliable market valuations were virtually impossible due to inactivity on the markets.

In response, the IASB introduced an amendment on 13 October 2008 to IAS 39 *"Financial Instruments: Recognition and Measurement"* and to IFRS 7 *"Financial Instruments: Disclosure"* without following regular procedures. In November 2008, an additional amendment was issued, clarifying the technical details and stating the effective date of the new regulation. As a result, a substantial share of assets was reclassified, which had a positive impact on key financial indicators and regulatory capital. Although profits were recognized, fair value losses were only partially recognized. Consequently, until 2008 positive market value changes of such assets increased the equity of banks, but market value losses no longer affected the capital or Profit and Loss (PnL) once the asset was reclassified. AfS securities are a significant component of bank balance sheet assets.

In short, the amendment enabled the financial industry to negate losses in amounts of hundreds of billions of euros.[21]

The main goal is to assess the overall impact of the FVA, in particular, the concept of Other Comprehensive Income (OCI), on banks' financial statements, and if the new Basel III regulations capture this critical factor sufficiently (for example, in regards to prudential filters). Moreover, this book aims to increase awareness among regulators and investors about the concept of OCI.

---

[18] Kholmy, 2012. P.20; Fiechter, 2009. P.1.
[19] Laux / Leuz, 2010. P.1.
[20] Institute of International Finance, 2008. P.2; Kholmy, 2012. P.2.
[21] Kholmy / Ernstberger, 2012. P.21.

The OCI includes items of income and expenses that are not recognized (IAS 1.7) in income statements, but increase or decrease a bank's equity. These items also include income and expenses from AfS positions in accordance with IAS 39.

The results of this research are relevant, since it explores the consequences of OCI accounting in times of declining market prices and underpins the fact that an amendment to IAS 39 was indispensable. Banks reclassified assets from FV-categories to other categories, where it is allowed to value the assets at cost or amortized cost in order to prevent a regulatory undercapitalization."[22]

1.1 Research questions

1.1.1 Does the concept of OCI allow capital to leave the bank, although gains have not yet been realized?

Critics made the FVA accounting responsible for (at the very least viewed it as being a catalyst) contributing to the intensity of the recent financial crisis.[23] This presumption is clearly visible in the amendment to IAS 39 issued by IASB, which modified the application of FVA for financial instruments *"...in order to prevent further asset write-offs"*.[24]

This book will primarily focus on banks in Europe that comply with IFRS, specifically those who reclassified assets in accordance with the amendment. Critics claim that the amendment is clearly favourable for banks due to the strong lobbying behind the amendment and its hasty release.[25]

As regards the concept of OCI, the IAS 39 amendment combined with IFRS 7 opened an opportunity to create transparency about the differences of using OCI compared to PnL accounting.

1.1.2 Is the poor capitalization of several banks also a result of the IFRS's OCI concept?

During the course and in the aftermath of the recent financial crisis, the rules for FVA have been heavily criticized, in particular, its contribution to financial losses.

Critics further argue, that the incapacity to value assets, especially in illiquid markets, creates a decline in confidence among market participants. They argue that there is the necessity *"to correct the unintended consequences of mark-to-market accounting, especially related to determining fair*

---

[22] Kholmy / Ernstberger, 2012. P.22
[23] Wallison, 2008; Forbes, 2009. P.41.
[24] Kholmy, 2012. P.22.
[25] Kholmy, 2012. P.22.

value for illiquid assets in unstable markets, and the need for enhanced transparency in the form of more meaningful disclosures."[26]

The IFRS concept of the OCI or fair value accounting definitely was not the sole cause of the credit crisis.[27] However, OCI created a domino effect, accelerating the decline of market values in an unstable market.[28] In the worst-case scenario, this could have resulted in a *"downward death spiral for financial companies large and small."*[29]

A large amount of assets is measured at FV and prior to the recent financial crisis, financial companies even had a much larger share of fair valued assets.[30]

It can be concluded that financial institutions like investment banks, which measure assets at FV, had to suffer more than, for example, commercial ones, which were not reporting at FV to the same extent.[31]

During the financial crisis, the effect of declining market values was tremendous. Bank's for example valued up to 80% of their financial assets at FV in 2008.[32]

In 2008, BNY Mellon[33], as an example, reported security losses of USD 1.6 billion. This major loss was recorded in the firm's Other Comprehensive Income (OCI). The *"unrealized"* losses recorded in OCI in fact amounted to USD 4.1 billion on 31 December 2008 for 2008 alone. The explanation BNY Mellon provided was as follows:[34]

"The ongoing disruption in the fixed income securities market has resulted in additional impairment charges, as well as an increase in unrealized securities losses. In 2008, we recorded impairment charges on our securities portfolio of $1.6 billion... These losses were primarily driven by lower market values of Alt-A, home equity lines of credit and asset-backed collateralized debt obligations securities. The market value of these securities was severely impacted by the depressed housing market and deterioration in the broader economy. The unrealized loss on the securities

---

[26] Casabona / Shoaf, 2010. P.20.
[27] Gingrich, 2008. P.25.
[28] Gingrich, 2008. P.25.
[29] Gingrich, 2008. P.25
[30] Casabona / Shoaf, 2010. P.21.
[31] Casabona / Shoaf, 2010. P.21.
[32] Zion, 2009. P.3.
[33] Casabona / Shoaf, 2010; BNY Mellon is a financial institution (part of S&P 500). It was formed by a merger of The Bank of New York which previously acquired JPMorgan Chase's Corporate Trust business with Mellon Financial Corporation into BNY Mellon finally.
[34] Casabona / Shoaf, 2010. P.21.

portfolio, which is recorded in **other comprehensive income**, was $4.1 billion at Dec. 31, 2008, compared with $342 million at Dec. 31, 2007."

It is true that those losses were unrealized. However, the relevant question in this regard is what happened to the unrealized profits that were recorded in OCI in the years before the crisis, which were obviously not sustainable. If such unrealized profits had left the bank, for example as dividend payments or bonuses, the poor capitalization of this bank would also be a result of the IFRS's concept of OCI.

It should be mentioned here that several banks implemented the total return/revenue approach in their internal reporting and that bonus payments were, for example, determined on the basis of total revenues including market value changes of AfS positions recorded in OCI. This means that capital which was never earned left the bank, and capitalization weakened as a consequence.

1.1.3 Has the problem been properly addressed by European regulators, in particular in terms of prudential filters?

One question that remains unanswered is the potential impact of the reclassification on regulatory capital. Banks can now report a financial instrument that previously was valued at fair value at amortized cost instead. If the findings of this study reveal that regulatory capital might be decreased because unrealized profits are leaving the bank (considering they are not deducted from regulatory capital, regulators will need to react. Information about reclassifications must be disclosed in the footnotes of financial statements.

1.2 Definitions

1.2.1 Financial instruments

Such instruments include a broad range of financial assets and liabilities. Financial instruments include primary financial instruments (shares, etc.) and derivative financial instruments (forwards, interest rate swaps, options, futures, Credit Default Swaps, etc.).[35]

1.2.2 Other Comprehensive Income (OCI)

OCI contains the gains and losses on the FV re-measurements, which are arising out of AfS financial assets and the share of gains and losses on hedges.[36]

---

[35] Audit Committee Institute, 2012. P. 76.
[36] IAS 39.

In addition, it covers the adjustments on retained earnings and the revaluation surplus for example.[37]

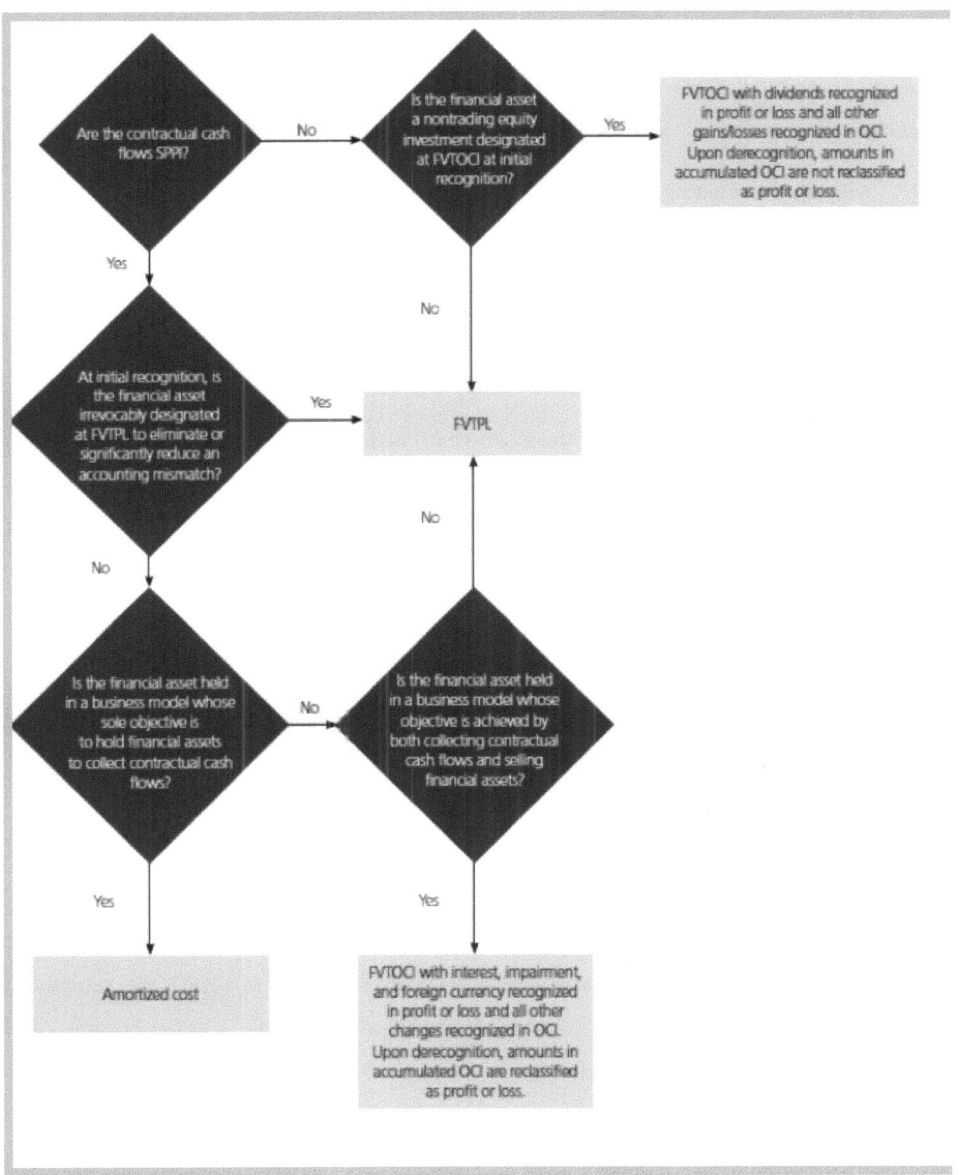

Graph 1: OCI source: iasplus.com (http://www.iasplus.com/en/images/old/publications/united-states/heads-up/vol-21-issue-20-1, 13.04.2016)

---

[37] IAS 16, 19, 21, 38.

1.2.3 Fair value (FV)

The best indicator of FV is a published price quotation within a liquid active market. In case such an indicator is not available, valuation techniques can be used to determine it. The objective in this case is to establish a market exchange on the measurement date under normal business conditions.[38]

1.2.4 Fair value accounting (FVA)

Under IFRS, FVA refers to a market-based measurement technique. It was first used in IAS 16, Accounting for Property, Plant and Equipment. IAS 16 defines a fair value as:[39]

"... the amount for which an asset could be exchanged or a liability settled between knowledgeable, willing parties in an arm's length transactions."[40]

The standard relies on a valuation of the asset, which is close to the market price in aliquid and active market. In case of an uncertain fair value (due to the lack of an active market), many banks, in particular large ones, rely on models calculating the net present value based on techniques estimating expected future cash flows.[41]

1.2.5 Financial crisis

In a financial crisis, the value of assets or financial institutions drops sharply. Significant decreases in prices are often made possible by previous disproportionate increases. Such a crisis is often associated with a panic, bank runs and irrational investor behaviour. Investors often hastily sell off assets or rapidly withdraw their savings, expecting the value to decrease even further otherwise. An emerging crisis is in many cases preceded by an overvaluation of assets. Only a vague consensus exists on the origins and possibilities to prevent financial crises.[42]

1.2.6 Recent financial crisis

The recent crisis (the credit and financial market crisis which began in mid-2007) was caused by a subprime mortgage crisis in the US real estate market, which became a global financial crisis. Investment banking was especially affected. When banks had to suffer immense losses on their

---

[38] Audit Committee Institute, 2012. P. 82.
[39] Kholmy, 2012. P.15.
[40] IAS 16.6; Kholmy, 2012.P.15
[41] SEC, 2008. P. 4.
[42] Fiechter, 2012. P.31.

subprime positions, investors became reluctant to hold such assets. As a consequence, markets became illiquid and FV deteriorated.[43]

The resent crisis still is considered as the most severe global cyclical downturn since 1933.[44] However, it also provides the opportunity of examining the consequences of the concept of OCI within a volatile environment. To date, most of the relevant studies have merely focused on a controversy about whether FVA is to blame for the onset of the crisis[45] and what the effects on the banking industry are.[46]

As a result of FVA and the concept of OCI implemented in IFRS, the crisis led to unimaginable write-offs in financial institutions.

A significant share of banks' balance sheets consisted of financial instruments and the banking sector was therefore particularly vulnerable. Hence, there was a high risk of considerable write-downs in bearish markets, which became a reality during the recent crisis.

This put an enormous pressure on the IASB. Its response was the amendment to IAS 39. This provided banks with the possibility to value assets at amortized costs where no active market exists or where it disappears. Furthermore, it resolved inconsistencies between accounting rules of US GAAP and IFRS.[47]

1.2.7 Regulatory capital

Regulatory capital generally consists of the components as follows:

Tier 1 Capital
a. Common Equity Tier 1
b. Additional Tier 1
2. Tier 2 Capital (gone-concern capital)

Table 1: Components of regulatory capital[48]

---

[43] Ryan, 2008. P.1605.
[44] Kholmy Guest, 2011; Hall, 2010. P.113.
[45] Laux / Leuz, 2010. P.826.
[46] Fiechter / Novotny-Farkas, 2011; Song et al., 2010; Vyas, 2011. P.22.
[47] IASB, 2008. P.7.
[48] BIS, 2010. P.4.

For each category, a single set of criteria is in place that instruments are "*required to meet before inclusion in the relevant category.*"[49]

1.2.8 Regulatory adjustments

Regulatory adjustments shall be applied to regulatory capital. They are applied in the calculation of Common Equity Tier 1 (CET1).[50]

1.2.9 Prudential filters

The European Banking Authority (EBA)[51] recommends prudential filters as correction factors for IFRS reported equity of credit institutions. They are generally necessary because the scope of IFRS is not in line with the mandate of regulators. The purpose of IFRS financial statements is to provide useful information for investor decision-making. This is therefore not consistent with the tasks of banking supervision, which is primarily to guarantee the functioning of the financial system and creditor protection. The prudential filter takes into account valuation consequences of the FVA through a reconciliation of IFRS equity to regulatory capital. The initial idea was that prudential filters, applied in the calculation of regulatory capital, would filter out unrealized gains or losses from the FVA of assets. The objective was to achieve consistent creditor protection by ensuring the sustainability and durability of own funds items. It sought to safeguard the risk buffer function of own funds. The concept of prudential filters was first introduced in 2004 in the document of CEBS "*Guidelines on Prudential Filters for Regulatory Capital*" and was the result of meetings of Banking Supervisors.[52]

1.2.10 Prudential valuation and prudential filter

The commonality between these two approaches is that they reduce regulatory capital. However, they pursue different goals. Valuation adjustments are based on Tier 1 (CET) capital, while prudential filters can be used for all categories of regulatory capital. In this regard, the interface between the two approaches is essential, as financial instruments classified as AfS could, theoretically, lie within the scope of both approaches. Another commonality they have is that EBA questioned the value of equity positions on behalf of the EU Commission.

---

[49] BIS, 2010. P.12.
[50] EBF, 2013. P.5.
[51] Formerly Committee of European Banking Supervisors (CEBS).
[52] CEBS; Guidelines on Prudential Filters for Regulatory Capital, 2004.

For example, if a positive revaluation reserve indicated during the financial crisis that its ability to absorb losses was insufficient, EBA consequently requested components of common equity to be made available in full and directly for immediate coverage of risks and losses.[53]

This book focuses in particular on prudential filters in the context of OCI, and how they will affect primarily banks with a positive revaluation reserve. However, different point of views should be considered when examining the possible interaction between prudential filters and prudent valuation:[54]

- While prudent valuation addresses the entire valuation of assets, a prudential filter only applies to unrealized gains.
- As prudent valuation adjustments would result in an adjustment of CET1, prudential filters may result in a partial recognition of all equity categories, as already discussed, or may not be included at all.

1.3 Distribution Policy of Banks

A sustainable distribution policy implies building up sufficient reserves in order to have sufficient capital in times of crisis. However, during times of crisis, banks in the past have distributed as much earnings as possible. According to the Bank for International Settlements (BIS), the central bank of all central banks, and based on a sample of 90 large banks from different continents, alone between 2007 and 2014, i.e. after the financial crisis, banks distributed aporoximately EUR 1.7 thousand billion to their shareholders. This amount was paid out as dividends and share buy-backs mainly, and does not include any bonus payments to employees.[55]

On the other hand, during the same period, only about 25% of this amount (EUR 405 billion) was retained to strengthen the capital base. This means that retained earnings, which represent a key source of bank capital, would have been 75% higher if profits had been ploughed back into the banks.[56]

According to Hyun Song Shin, chief economist of the BIS in Basel, banks prioritize profit distribution over building up reserve – even in times of crisis. He strongly criticized banks'

---

[53] CRR Article 26 (1).
[54] EBA, 2013, consultation paper on prudent valuation. P.4.
[55] Braunberger, 2016. P.2.
[56] Shin, 2016. P.2.

behaviour in this regard. The aim of the bank capital is to absorb losses in the sense that the bank's own funds can absorb the losses.[57]

The most relevant part of banks' own funds are retained earnings, which represent the stock of profits that have not been disbursed. The following graph presents the sum of retained earnings of a sample of 90 euro-area banks and the total sums disbursed only as dividends since 2007:[58]

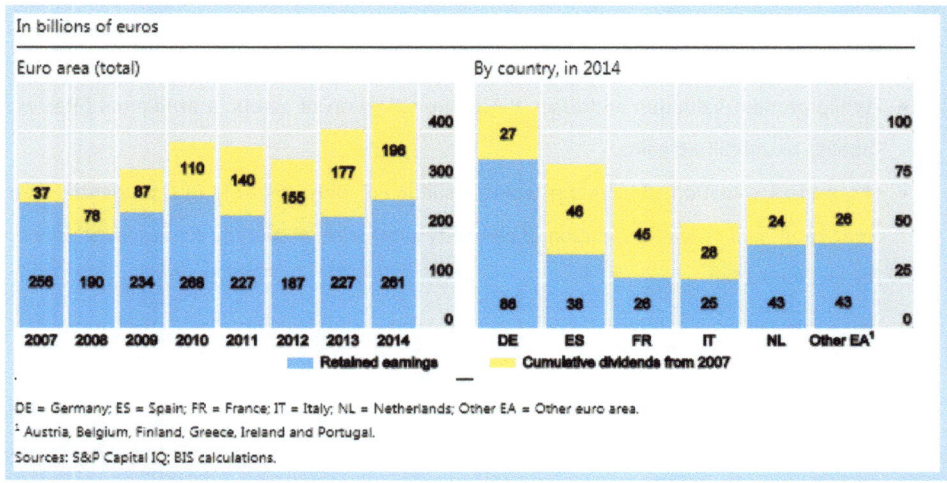

Chart 1: Cumulative dividends of 90 European banks since the crisis (Source: Shin, 2016)

Looking at the blue bars, representing the sum of retained earnings, it is noticeable that they significantly declined. This occurs when a bank suffers losses and has to compensate this by the retained earnings. In 2014, the total amount of those retained earnings dropped to EUR 261 billion and the total dividends since 2007 reached EUR 196 billion. It can be concluded that the regulatory capital would have been significantly higher, in case the banks had chosen to retain the profits in their capital instead disbursing them as dividends.[59]

Assuming that a larger sum of retained earnings would support *"...a virtuous circle of greater lending and higher profits, the hypothetical increase in retained earnings might have been even larger..."*.[60]

---

[57] Shin, 2016. P.2.
[58] Shin, 2016. P.3.
[59] Shin, 2016. P.3.
[60] Shin, 2016. P.3.

It has to be pointed out, that the accumulated dividends of banks from Spain, Italy and France even exceeded retained earnings. They would have been increased by 100% if the profits would not have left the banks.[61]

The following graph illustrates the fact, that the amount of banks having negative retained earnings even increased in 2011, and that there are now even more as in comparison to 2007:

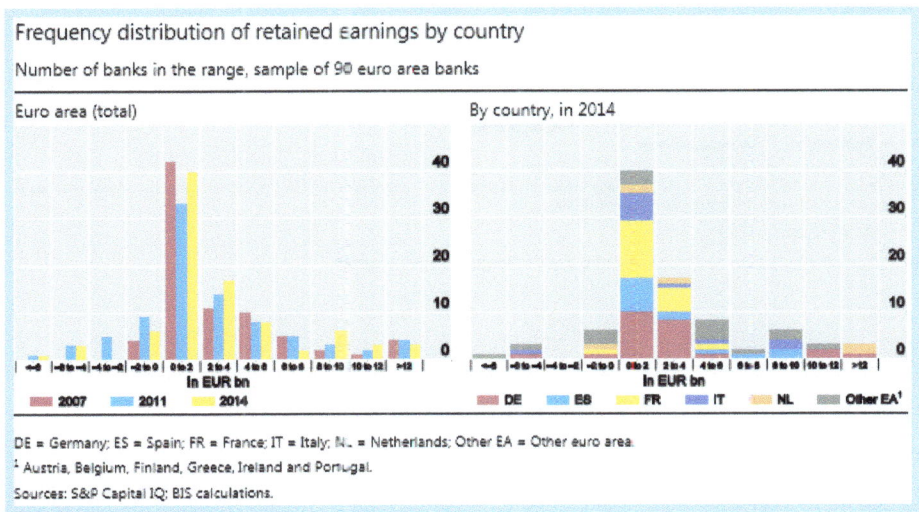

Chart 2: Frequency distribution of retained earnings by country 2014

The capital of banks (heir own funds) is of upmost importance. A BIS report describes the implications of the amount own funds on lending. It contains a larger sample of banks (105) in advanced economies and concludes that for usual amounts of leverage, *"banks could go a long way towards mitigating their supposedly higher cost of equity funding by keeping back more of their profits for retained earnings..."*.[62]

---

[61] Shin, 2016. P.4.
[62] Shin, 2016. P.2.

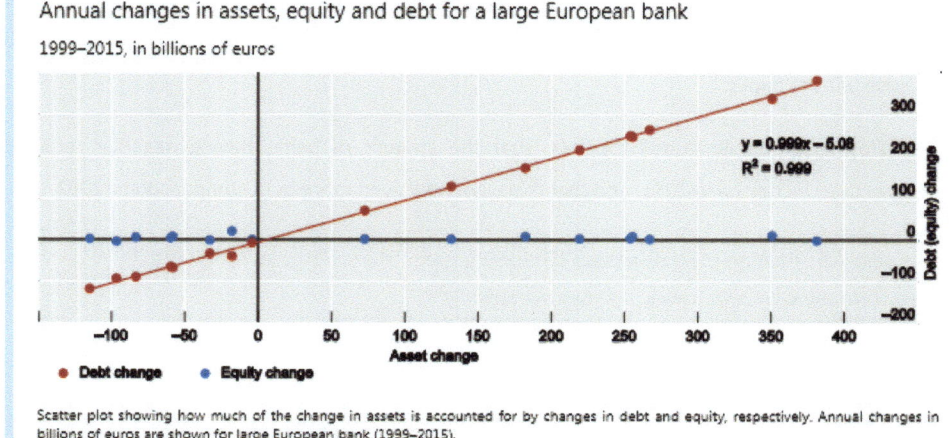

Chart 3: Annual changes in assets, equity and debt of large European banks

It is evident that the increase in asset volume was funded by debt, whereby the banks' own funds did not increase. Therefore, banks increased their total assets by increasing their leverage. Problems are likely in case the financial outlook worsen and the financial institution is no longer in the position to secure the refinancing.

BIS examined why banks applying strategies eroding their regulatory capital in such amounts and why they are reluctant to increase their capital base by the recorded profits. BIS questioned whether there are *"...possible tensions between the private interests of some bank stakeholders versus the wider public interest of maintaining a soundly functioning banking system that can supply credit in support of economic activity..."*.[63]

Banks disbursed very high dividends after the crisis. Therefore, regulators should be concerned, since soundly capitalized banks are a public good. The interests of the public and stakeholders of banks may diverge. A proper set of regulations must therefore guarantee that banks have a sufficient amount of regulatory capital. It should be of major concern for central banks in line with their mandate for financial stability, to have soundly capitalized banks.

BIS criticizes the generous distribution of money: *"If you feel restricted by the regulatory banks that retained earnings instead of dividends on a solution to the problem makes. From the point of*

---

[63] Shin, 2016, P.3.

view of the public interest, this is better than the loosening of regulations, which invites you to a higher level of debt." Banks often claim that high dividends are unavoidable if shareholders are to be kept satisfied in a difficult environment, as institutional shareholders face competitors on quarterly results, for example, and therefore have an interest in high cash distributions, even if this is not sustainable.[64]

However, with the RTS on prudential valuation, a loosening of regulations allowing banks to have a higher level of debt is already underway.

1.4 Overview IAS/IFRS systematic

1.4.1 IAS 39 – Financial instruments: recognition and measurements

In this context, the standard initially focused on measuring and recognizing financial instruments. A financial instrument can be classified into four categories after they are acquired:[65]

- *"Fair value through PnL"*, which has two subcategories: *"HfT"* and *"designed by entity as fair value through profit or loss"*
- *"Held-to-maturity"*
- *"Loans and receivables"*
- AfS.

In order to get allocated to HfT, the intention of holding this asset or the liability is to realize profits by trading in the near future. Derivatives can also be allocated to this category. In addition, FV through profit or loss classification can be applicable to such assets (certain conditions must be met). There is only one precondition and that is the existence of an active market. The *"Held-to-maturity"* category mainly includes non-derivate assets that were held *"with the intention and ability"* to keep *"the asset until maturity"*. Finally, these non-derivate assets having fixed payments and which are not quotable from an active market, are allocated to the *"Loans and receivables"* category.[66]

---

[64] Braunberger, 2016. P.3.
[65] IAS 39.
[66] IAS 39.

For the OCI, the category AfS is the most important. This category is designated to all non-derivate financial assets which cannot be classified in another categorie.[67] Therefore, this category represents all the remaining positions.

This broad definition implies that the amount of financial assets allocated to this category is significant in practice. Prior to and during the crisis, banks mainly allocated their structured credit products (ABS, etc.) to this category. These structured credit products were precisely those products that experienced an outrageous drop in market value as the markets almost disappeared and investors became reluctant to buy these toxic assets.

The valuation of each of these categories differs. The approach to FV through PnL is needless to say based on FV and visible in PnL. Loans and receivables and held-to-maturity are valued at amortized cost.

What is noteworthy and especially relevant for this paper (i.e. relevant for OCI) is the category AfS. The PnL for this category is based on FV through equity measurement. Gains and losses in are only charged to the equity of a bank and recorded (parked) in OCI.

The market value changes of these positions are recognized within the OCI only, without any effect on PnL, as these were unrealized and only parked within the OCI revaluation reserve. This means that they only have an impact on the equity of a bank without affecting PnL. Before the crisis, business lines active in the structured credit business registered huge amounts of unrealized profits. Those profits increased banks' equity, although the recent crisis ruthlessly demonstrated that it was a bubble only and that the values were not sustainable and were never realized in an arm's length transaction.

---

[67] IAS 39.

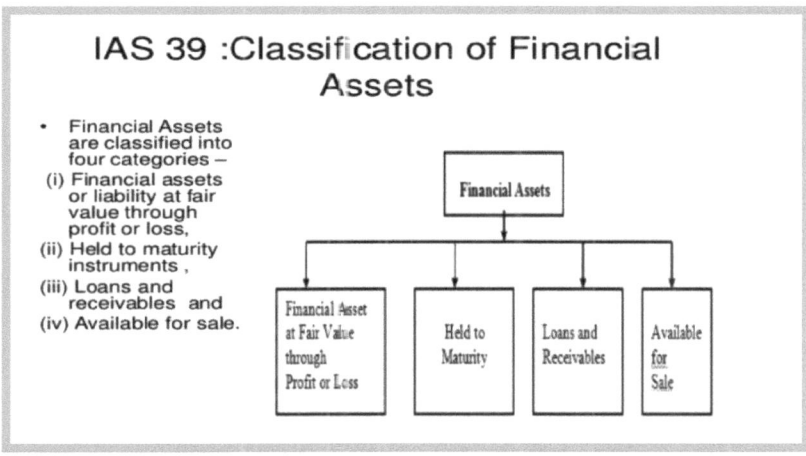

Chart 4: IAS 39 Classification of Financial Assets (Source: Ghosh, 2013)

1.4.2 IFRS for financial instruments

On October 13th 2008, at the peak of the crisis, an amendment to the old standard IAS 39 was issued by IASB. It was a response to a request by the EU on October 7th 2008.[68] In a meeting on October 6th 2008, the Economic Council of the EU decided that IFRS shall address the difference in the accounting approach to asset classification with US GAAP as soon as possible. The reclassification of assets enabled banks under US GAAP to value their assets at purchase price and not FV. The underlying idea behind this was that by avoiding any reporting of market prices in an extremely volatile market could stabilize the banks by negating the losses they were facing.[69]

1.4.3 Fair value accounting – a critical evaluation

Since 2005, all companies listed in the EU are obliged to publish financial reports in accordance with IFRS. This meant a sharp contrast (local, GAAP, etc.) to using amortization costs compared to the standards previously applied.[70]

Supporters claim that FVA was beneficial to investors as it provides more insight to the risk profile. Having said that, FVA could foster market discipline and improve asset allocation.[71] This concept makes most sense, however, if market quotes are available.

---

[68] EU, 2008.
[69] Amendment to IAS 39, 2008.
[70] Laux / Leuz, 2009. P.826.
[71] Platin / Sapra / Shin, 2008. P.435.

Alternatively, the best available estimate exercising judgement about methods and assumptions can be used.[72] Antagonists of FVA argue that financial reporting might be less reliable when no efficient market is in place. Reliability decreases if the valuation is based on assumptions.[73] A potential unreliability of assumptions and models would not be transparent to outside investors. Opponents further point out that fair value accounting has pro-cyclical effects.[74] This is largely based on the fact that trading is pro-cyclical, which causes destabilizing effects on prices and results in an increase of asset volatility. This is mainly relevant for portfolios consisting of senior and long-term illiquid assets.[75] Due to the accounting rules and methods, changes in fair value do not necessarily represent underlying economics. Besides underlying economic volatility, mixed measurement accounting models and fair value estimations cause changes in values as well.[76]

This means that management estimations are replacing an active market in times of market inactivity. The fair value is then based on assumptions and *not* on market prices.

This is by and large the case in every technique using estimations or assumptions.[77] There is broad consensus that FVA accelerated the crisis.[78] However, some authors disagree with this assertion pointing out the different objectives of regulators and accounting standard setters.[79]

Banks' investments were funded by assets pledged as collateral. Those assets only had a high market value in bullish markets. When banks were forced to lower their valuations, the losses were charged to their equity.[80] As the (allegedly) earned profits derived from previously estimated or observed fair values left the banks—at least in part—as bonuses or dividends, banks had problems maintaining their solvency ratios during and after the crisis. This is the case until today as many of the relevant banks still have poor capital ratios. This also became obvious in the course of the comprehensive assessment performed by the ECB before taking over the mandate to supervise significant banks in Europe. It also became transparent with the recent stress test results of the stresstest perforemed by the EBA.

---

[72] Glavan, 2010. P.55.
[73] ECB, 2004.
[74] ECB, 2004.
[75] Platin, 2008. P.435.
[76] Barth, 2004. P.33.
[77] Barth, 2004. P.33.
[78] De la Dehesa, 2009. P.3.
[79] Barth / Landsman, 2010. P.13.
[80] Glavan, 2010. P.55.

After and during the recent financial crisis, banks were left with only few possibilities and the most obvious one was only hypothetical: raising additional capital under such turbulent market conditions was not advisable. Also the sale of assets was not a viable solution, as it would have resembled fire sales. The result would have been enormous realized losses. Several banks reduced lending, which had a negative impact on the economy and increased NPL ratios.

Based on the "American Bankers Association", balance sheets were also contaminated due to FVA.[81]

Research shows that certain key indicators have been improved since the amendment to IAS 39. However, this only improved banks' situation accounting wise and had of course nothing to do with the underlying economic factors.[82]

Although accounting values improved and assets were no longer valued mark-to-market, banks remained strongly exposed to market risks. This became apparent at the latest when a large number of reclassifying banks requested support from the government.[83] Those banks that reclassified assets also had lower capital adequacy ratios and were therefore more at risk of breaching the minimum capital requirements.[84]

---

[81] American Bankers Association, 2008; Wallison, 2008; Whallen, 2008.
[82] Fietcher, 2011. P.22
[83] Fietcher, 2011. P.22.
[84] Paanen/ Renders/ Shima, 2012. P.50.

2 AMENDEMENT TO IAS 39 AND IFRS 7

The amendment to IAS 39 and IFRS 7 was published on October 13th 2008.

2.1 What the amendment changed

This amendment allowed the reclassification of the categories[85]

- *"Held for trading"* and
- *"Available for sale"*

in

- *"Held to maturity"* or
- from *"Held for trading"* to *"Available for sale"* or
- to *"Loans and receivables"*.

Every category has is own valuation method. It must be pointed out that by reclassifying from a category valued at fair value, banks could value their financial instruments at historical costs. IFRS 7 was issued to ensure transparency on the impacts of reclassifications (disclosure in financial reports, etc.).

Such mutations in accounting principles of course also entail an impact on regulatory capital. Evidence has already shown that banks used the amendment in an opportunistic manner.[86]

Suddenly, banks were provided with the opportunity to reallocate AfS-instruments to Loans and Receivables (LaR).[87] This means that positions that had previously been measured FV could now be valued alternatively at amortized cost and subsequently banks were allowed to correct losses, which had already been reported internally, retroactively as of July 1st 2008, considering that the amendment came into effect retroactively as of this date.[88]

---

[85] Paanen / Renders / Shima, 2012. P.50.
[86] Fietcher, 2011. P.20.
[87] Kholmy / Ernstberger, 2012. P.15.
[88] IAS 39.103

In accordance with IAS 39, the amendment allows reclassifying AfS instruments in LaR under the precondition *"that the bank has the intention and ability to hold that financial asset"*. The new value was determined by the FV as of the reclassification date.[89]

Because the IASB allowed a reallocation of assets out of FV, banks had additional flexibility, allowing the management of earnings by minimizing FV losses.[90]

The *EESA- Emergency Economic Stabilization Act* was enacted as early as October 3rd 2008. The act is also known as the bailout of US financial system. EESA authorized the US Secretary of Treasury to buy distressed assets, in particular asset-backed securities and I addition to inject capital into banks. The budget amounted to up to USD 700 billion.

The asset purchases were performed through the so-called Troubled Asset Relief Program (TARP). The objectives of TARP were to stabilize the economy, protect taxpayers, preserve homeownership, strong oversight and the elimination of windfalls for executives.[91]

As market value changes recorded within OCI were unrealized, those profits or losses were realized all of a sudden when these assets were purchased through TARP, although they were never sold in an arm's length transaction, as private investors were very reluctant to buy such assets. They even referred to structured credit products as toxic assets.

If the fair value was overestimated at the time of reclassification, unjustified profits were realized with the purchases through TARP. This was like a cross-subsidization of the finance industry.

There may have been no alternative to this approach at the time. However, regulators should ensure that unrealized profits do *not* lead to a capital drain in the future. One way to assure this is to make OCI subject to a prudential filter and to deduct it from regulatory capital.

As another consequence, EESA required SEC to carry out a study of mark-to-market accounting. The scope was as follows:[92]

- Impact of accounting standards on the failure of banks
- The Process used by the FASB for the development of accounting standards
- Alternatives or adjustments to the existing standards.

---

[89] IAS 39. 50.
[90] IAS 39.
[91] Casabona / Shoaf, 2010. P.21.
[92] Casabona / Shoaf, 2010. P.21.

The *"Study on Mark-to-Market Accounting"*[93] was completed in December 2008 and submitted to the US Congress on 30 December 2008. The following key issues were addressed:[94]

- Effect of FVA on banks balance sheets
- Effect of FVA on financial institutions failures in 2008
- Process the FASB follows to develop accounting standards
- Alternatives to FVA standards
- Advisability and feasibility of modifications to FVA standards.

Thy concluded that mark-to-market accounting should not be changed for the time eing, as an abrupt change would destroy investor confidence in IFRS. The study makes several recommendations, such as the improvement of FVA requirements, and addresses the need to clarify the valuation of assets. Beginning with the year 2009, the recent financial crisis intensified. The economy headed towards a very deep recession and criticism of this practice increased. As a response, the FASB completed several credit crisis projects on that topic as follows:[95]

- Determining FV *"...when the volume and level of activity for the asset or liability have significantly decreased and identifying transactions that are not orderly."*[96]
- Interim disclosures about FVA
- Recognition and presentation of other-than-temporary Impairment
- Measuring liabilities
- Investment in certain entities that calculate "net asset value per share".

Subsequently, new guidelines[97] provided additional direction on appraising the FV in case "volume and level of activity significantly decrease, and on identifying transactions that are not orderly."[98]

The FASB offers support to carefully evaluate whether the volume has decreased compared to "normal market conditions". Such an assessment must consider the following factors:[99]

---

[93] Casabona / Shoaf, 2010. P.22
[94] Casabona / Shoaf, 2010. P.22; Barth, 2010. P.3
[95] Casabona / Shoaf, 2010. P.22
[96] Casabona / Shoaf, 2010. P.22

[97] FSP FAS 157-4.
[98] Casabona / Shoaf, 2010. P.24
[99] Casabona / Shoaf, 2010. P.24

- Only very few recent deals based on volume in the market
- The price quotations are not based on the availale current information
- The price quotations vary substantially, either over time or among market makers
- Significant grow of "implied l quidity risk premiums, yields, or performance indicators."
- Significant drop in or even absence of a market for new issuances.

If such factors are present, FASB recommends applying another technique for valuation:[100] *"The reporting entity shall consider the reasonableness of the range of FV estimates"*[101]

With regard to OCI, FASB states that not credit related losses on held-to-maturity assets, which are reported within the OCI, will be reversed. It should clearly not result in an increase of earnings. Instead, the discount shall be aggregated back through OCI, which is the not credit related amount of held-to-maturity assets recorded in OCI, shall be amortized over the lifetime after deductions as increasing OCI and the investment balance.[102]

The impact of this new announcement is that reclassifications or changes in valuation techniques become more likely in case the markets become illiquid. In liquid markets, financial instruments are measured at FV as long as prices go up. However, when it becomes apparent that it is only a bubble and the markets subsequently become illiquid, the losses in FV are no longer recognized. This is like an accounting arbitrage and the bank's regulatory capital would contain values that cannot be realized in an arm's length transaction. This means they are no longer realistic.

---

[100] Orrick, 2011. P.19.
[101] Casabona / Shoaf, 2010. P.24
[102] Casabona / Shoaf, 2010. P.25

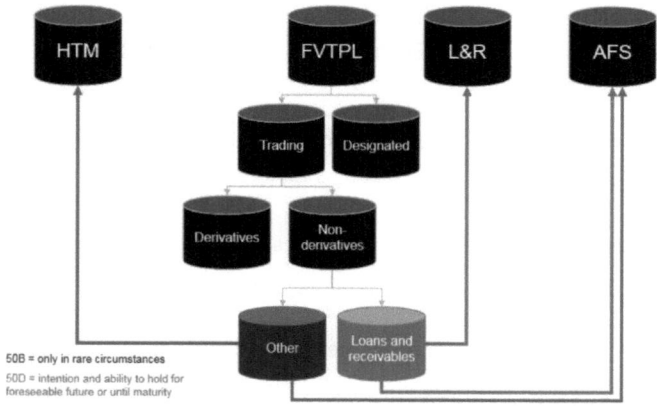

Chart 5: Overview of reclassification options (source: Bianco: Gli strumenti finanziari. Strumenti finanziari – 2 Agenda Strumenti finanziari Iscrizione iniziale e valutazione successiva Impairment Derecognitio)

2.2 Impact of the amendment

In order to prevent additional, but also in order to adjust already occurred losses, European banks reclassified financial instruments. For example, the Deutsche Bank AG reclassified financial assets in the amount of EUR 33 billion and therefore also avoided losses amounting to EUR 3.2 billion.[103]

One of the reasons for introducing the amendment was harmonization between US GAAP and IFRS. However, such an option to reallocating assets retroactively never existed in this was in US GAAP. This provided banks the possibility to assess the impact on their financials and decide whether a reclassification will have a desirable effect. This is a major difference as it allowed banks to take an opportunistic approach and involved a form of accounting arbitrage. [104]

The value determining the amortization cost was FV on the date of the executed reclassification, when the entity reclassified instruments out of HfT or AfS. In general, already recognized gains and losses cannot be reversed. All previous deductions to equity should remain. This was not valid for the reallocation, which had been made before November 1st 2008. In this case, a backdating of the value to July 1st 2008 was possible. Therefore, the IASB allowed to **avoid charges to income and equity** by revaluating assets from FVA to amortization costs.[105]

---

[103] Deutsche Bank, Financial statement, 2008.
[104] Kilicer, 2010. P. 54.
[105] Zhan, 2013. P.11.

Reclassifications had different impacts. In case assets were reclassified from HfT to amortization costs, the value of those assets remained stable over time. In particular, during declining markets in 2008, this meant an advantage as equity was no longer directly affected.[106]

What is more interesting for this study is the second effect in case an HfT asset is reclassified to AfS. In that event, the asset is still priced at fair value. However, changes will—from that point on—be reported in OCI only. Therefore, the bank has the possibility to exclude the effect from the income statement.

What is most interesting in this regard is the reclassification from AfS in *"Loans and Receivables "* or in *"Held to Maturity"*. Before the amendment was issued, each of these categories had its own criteria for a reason.

The asset had to obey with the definition of *"Loans and Receivables"* before t could be allocated to this category. As a result, fair value accounting was suspended for the reclassified assets and amortization costs used instead. The only impact of the amendment to IFRS 7 was the need for additional disclosure requirements for reclassified assets.[107]

According to a sample taken from banks of the European Union, with a significant amount relevant assets on their balance sheets and which report their financials under IFRS[108], about 40% had reclassified assets.[109]

---

[106] Fietcher, 2011. P.22.
[107] Bischof / Bruggemann / Daske, 2012. P.41.
[108] Database "Bankscope", approx. 120 banks and equal to approx. 90% of cummulative totals assets of all banks within the EU.
[109] Fietcher, 2011; Bischof, 2012. P.20.

There were three major classification types[110]:

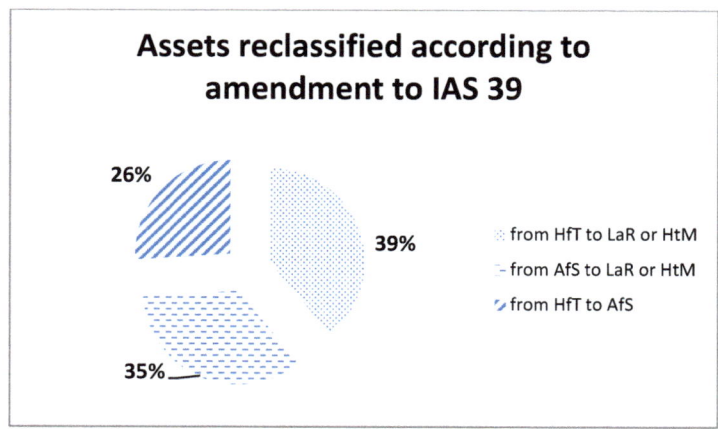

Chart 6: Assets reclassified as a result of amendment to IAS 39 (source: own picture based on data from database Bankscope)

The figure shows that approximately 74% was allocated to the categories *"LaR – Loans and Receivables"* and *"HtM – Held to Maturity"*, i.e. out of fair value accounting into amortization costs. Only about 26% was reclassified from *"HfT – held for Trading"* in *"AfS – Available for Sale"*. This means that shifts in fair value are no longer visible within the PnL, but in equity only. The recognisable system is as follows:

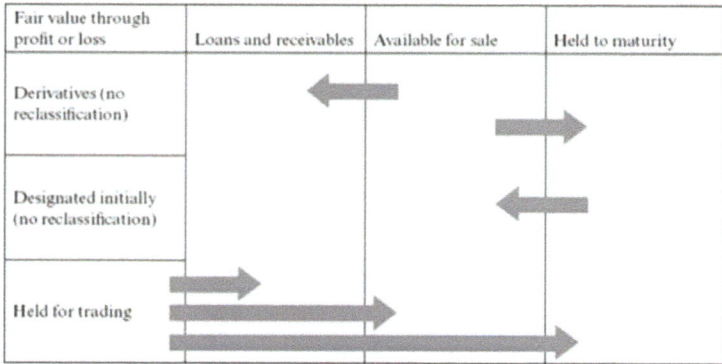

Chart 7: Recognizable System Reclassification IAS 39 (source: Wiley insights IFRS: Interpretation and Application of International Financial Reporting Standards)

---

[110] Multiple reclassifications possible.

3 THE ROLE OF OCI DURING THE RECENT FINANCIAL CRISIS

3.1 OCI and the recent crisis

The differences in FV from reclassified HfT to AfS assets were shifted from PnL to OCI. Therefore, it was mainly the financial reporting that changed as gains and losses of AfS positions affected the equity and were reported in OCI. The gains and losses from HfT positions are recognized within profit and loss accounts.

Presenting OCI items on performance statements, such as profit and loss accounts, increases judgement accuracy of financial statement users.[111]

When considering the situation during the recent crisis, the OCI was of highly important because the reallocation was often applied to prevent banks from going into bankruptcy.[112]

3.2 The impact on European banks

The reclassification had a tremendous impact on the regulatory capital and financials of European banks. Significant amounts of losses were not reported thanks to the reclassification. Based on net income, a relevant sample includes [113]

- Barclays
- Royal Bank of Scotland
- Societe Generale
- Credit Agricole
- Deutsche Bank AG (In 2011, reclassified assets from *financial assets at fair value through profit or loss* to *loans and receivables (L&R)* still amounted to EUR 6.7 billion).

An argument in favour of the reallocation was that the management emphasized that the aim is to hold the asset until maturity in order to collect all cash flows, but only in 2012 was an amount of approximately EUR 3 billion sold. Deutsche Bank AG provided the following argumentation:[114]

---

[111] Hirst / Hopkins, 1998. P.54.
[112] Fietcher, 2011. P.22.
[113] Papa, 2013. P.2.
[114] Deutsche Bank AG Financial Statement 2012; Papa, 2013. P.2.

"The aforementioned governance and approval process determined that assets sold were due to circumstances that were not foreseeable at the time of reclassification, including amendments to capital rules that led to higher capital requirements for the group as a whole,"

The question is how sustainable the intention of reclassification was at the time. The Lloyds Banking Group also faced several challenges. For example, in 2010, Lloyds reallocated government securities amounting to GBP 3.62 billion from AfS to HtM, and in 2012, government securities amounting to GBP 11.97 billion were reallocated from HtM to AfS due to managements shift of opinion not to hold it until maturity anymore.[115]

In June 2011, BNP Paribas reallocated assets amounting to EUR 6.3 to L&R. Disclosed was the strategy to hold these assets until maturity in order to be in the position to collect all cash flows. However, BNP Paribas was later forced to sell because of the greek bailout. [116]

These impacts demonstrate a challenge for regulators under such a framework, particularly when management intentions are subject to opportunistic changes.

---
[115] Papa, 2013. P.2.
[116] Papa, 2013. P.3.

4 CAPITAL REQUIREMENTS AND PRUDENTIAL FILTERS

4.1 The removal of prudential filters for unrealized gains and losses recognized in the revaluation reserve – AfS instruments as the largest contributor to changes to Tier 1 capital

To maintain a certain quality of own funds, prudential filters were initially introduced in 2004 by a CEBS guideline.[117] They targeted institutions using IAS/ IFRS for prudential reporting.

A study carried out by an Accounting Task Force of the Basel Committee[118] revealed that unrealized "gains and losses would have been the largest contributor of changes to Tier 1 capital during 2006 and 2011."[119]

Although it is difficult to understand the rationale behind it, the CRR, which became effective as of January 2014, removed the relevant prudential filters for the calculation of own funds, especially the prudential filter this book mainly focuses on: "**The prudential filter for unrealized gains and losses recognized in the revaluation reserve".** In the CRR a prudential filter for unrealized gains and losses from cash flow hedges respectively for changes in the value of liabilities due to changes in own credit risk remained.[120]

With the the CRR, which entered into force as a consequence of the financial crisis, maybe the most important prudential filter for the positions that caused the financial crisis and led to poor capitalization of banks was not strengthened, but even removed.

4.2 Treatment of AfS positions under the CEBS guideline 2004

For the AfS category, CEBS proposes applying the prudential filters to fair value revaluation reserves on AfS assets as follows:[121]

- *"For equities, unrealised losses should be deducted after tax from original own funds and unrealised gains should only partially be included in additional own funds before tax."*

---

[117] CEBS, 2004, Guidelines on prudential filters for regulatory capital.
[118] Wilch, 2015. P.24.
[119] Accounting Task Force of the Basel Committee, 2011. P.4.
[120] Basel Committee on Banking Supervision 2015, Working Paper 28. P.14.
[121] CEBS, 2004, Guidelines on prudential filters for regulatory capital. P.8.

- *"For loans and receivables, the unrealised gains and losses, apart from those related to impairment, are neutralised in own funds after tax."*
- *"For other available for sale assets, (for example debt securities, financial instruments subject to interest rate risk) two methods can be applied. According to the first one, items classified in this portfolio should be treated as equities, under the second method; they should be treated as loans and receivables."*[122]

4.3 Prudential filters and unrealized gains

Article 26(1) CRR clearly states that CET1 items shall only be recognized if available to the institution for *"unrestricted and immediate use to cover risks or losses as soon as these occur"*.[123]

Based on the developments after the financial crisis and on the discussions about FVA, serious concerns on unrealized gains on items measured at fair value are justified.

Obviously, it cannot be taken for granted that unrealized gains are available immediately to absorb losses when they arise. Due to negative impacts on market prices after the reporting date, these gains rapidly disappeared during the crisis when the markets became nearly illiquid. Such gains are only available from an accounting perspective to cover all current losses. However, we must adopt a prudential perspective, which means that CET1 items shall not only cover current, but also the risk of future losses.

However, unrealized gains *can* abruptly disappear in situations of distress. Consequently, unrealized gains cannot be taken into account to cover the risk of future losses. The regulators should be more than concerned when unrealized gains comprise a crucial amount of CET1. One has to take into account that buffers, which an entity built as a loss absorption capacity, consisted of unrealized gains. Having said that, a pro-cyclicality is obvious as market prices witness a downturn in crisis situations. Regulators should in fact even be concerned about the reliability of fair value measurement in general. This was presented in the course of the discussion about fair value accounting, particularly regarding level 2 and level 3 assets in accordance with IFRS 13.

---

[122] CEBS, 2004. Guidelines on prudential filters for regulatory capital. P.8.
[123] CRR, Article 26(1).

A logical consequence is to make such gains subject to a prudential filter and deduct them from regulatory capital under pillar I as well as II, as both the quality and amount of regulatory capital could be overstated in this position

4.4 Prudential filters CRR

In the CRR, the following articles are relevant:

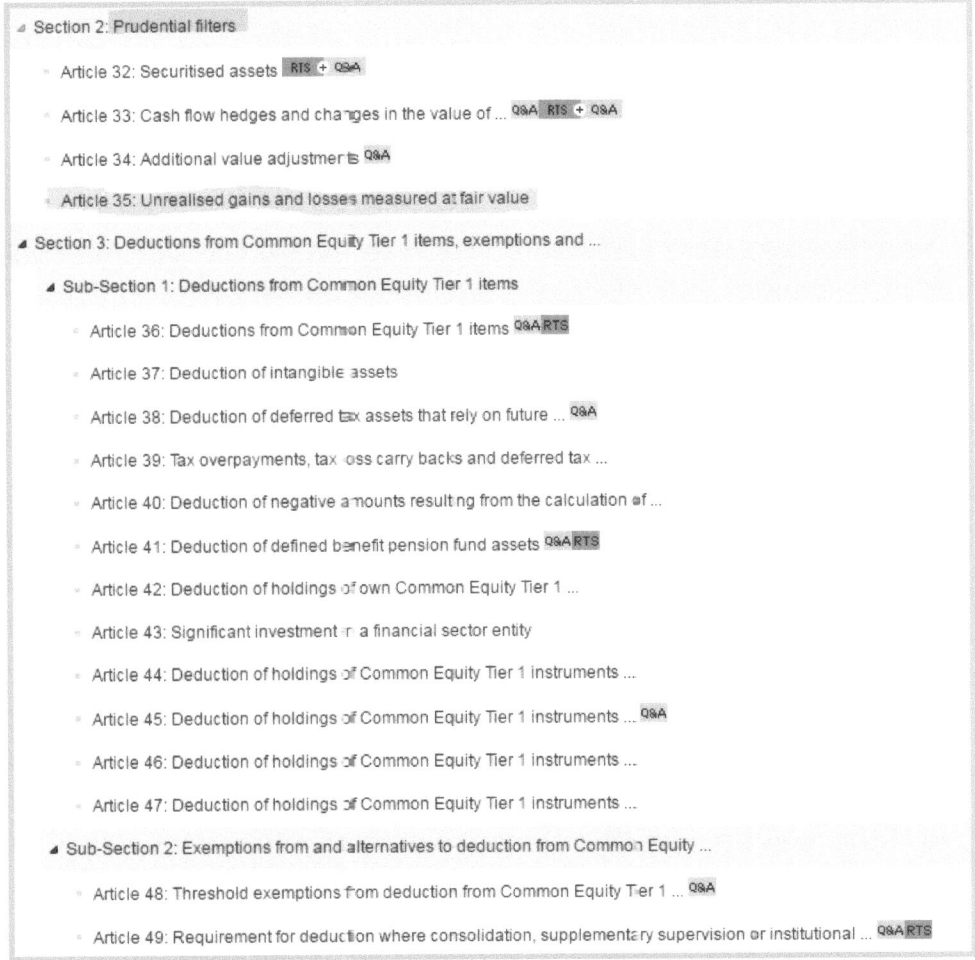

Chart 8: Prudential filters CRR relevant Articles (Source: https://www.eba.europa.eu/regulation-and-policy/single-rulebook/interactive-single-rulebook/-/interactive-single-rulebook/toc/504, 04.05.2016)

The most relevant article is Article 35 *"Unrealized gains and losses measured at fair value"*. Only cash flow hedges as stipulated in Article 33 *"...**shall not** make adjustments to remove from their own funds unrealised gains or losses on their assets or liabilities measured at fair value."* [124]

Path	Capital Requirements Regulation > PART TWO > TITLE I > CHAPTER 2 > Section 2 > Article 35 (Copy link to article)
Title	Article 35
Description	Unrealised gains and losses measured at fair value
Main content	Except in the case of the items referred to in Article 33, institutions shall not make adjustments to remove from their own funds unrealised gains or losses on their assets or liabilities measured at fair value.

Chart 9: Single Rule Book 2016 4 May: Description of Article 35 CRR

This means that CRR envisages the use of unrealized gains in equity without any adjustment (current treatment CRR).[125] Taking this fact into consideration, in particular that a revaluation reserve did not prove to have a sufficient loss absorption capacity, it is surprising that according to Article 35, *"institutions shall not make adjustments to remove unrealized gains or losses on their assets or liabilities from their own funds measured at fair value."*

Article 80(4) CRR requires *"...the EBA to provide technical advice to the Commission on possible treatments of unrealised gains measured at fair value other than including them in Common Equity Tier 1 without adjustment..."*[126] A EBA discussion paper states:

"The CRR also retains a prudential filter for unrealised gains and losses arising from cash flow hedges and for the changes in the value of liabilities (debt instruments and derivatives) due to changes in own credit risk (Article 33 of the CRR). The first filter has been introduced in the CRR in order to take into account the asymmetry in the accounting treatment of cash flow hedge transactions between the hedging instrument and the hedged item in cash flow hedges. The second is necessary to avoid the counter-intuitive effect that the level of own funds is conversely proportional to the credit quality of the institution itself. As these filters are prescribed by the CRR, the EBA has excluded them from the scope of the discussion paper and the technical advice."[127]

---

[124] CRR Article 35; EBA, 2013. P.8.
[125] EBA, 2013. P.8.
[126] CRR Article 80(4); EBA, 2013. P.8.
[127] EBA, 2013. P.8.

4.5 Basel III

The objective of Basel II is as follows:[128]

"The Basel Committee is raising the resilience of the banking sector by strengthening the regulatory capital framework, building on the three pillars of the Basel II framework. The reforms raise both the quality and quantity of the regulatory capital base and enhance the risk coverage of the capital framework. They are underpinned by a leverage ratio that serves as a backstop to the risk-based capital measures, is intended to constrain excess leverage in the banking system and provide an extra layer of protection against model risk and measurement error. Finally, the Committee is introducing a number of macroprudential elements into the capital framework to help contain systemic risks arising from procyclicality and from the interconnectedness of financial institutions."[129]

and

"It is critical that banks' risk exposures are backed by a high quality capital base. **The crisis demonstrated that credit losses and writedowns come out of retained earnings, which is part of banks' tangible common equity base.** *It also revealed the inconsistency in the definition of capital across jurisdictions and the lack of disclosure that would have enabled the market to fully assess and compare the quality of capital between institutions."*[130]

and

"Deductions from capital and prudential filters have been harmonised internationally and generally applied at the level of common equity or its equivalent in the case of non-joint stock companies. The remainder of the Tier 1 capital base must be comprised of instruments that are subordinated, have fully discretionary noncumulative dividends or coupons and have neither a maturity date nor an incentive to redeem."[131]

Part 1: Minimum capital requirements and buffers: *"...The global banking system* **entered the crisis with an insufficient level of high quality capital...**"[132]

---

[128] BIS, 2010. P.12.
[129] Basel Committee on Banking Supervision. Basel III, P. 2.
[130] BIS, 2010. P.12.
[131] BIS, 2010. P.12.
[132] BIS, 2010. P.21.

4.6 Outlook I: EBA Discussion Paper Prudential Filter, 2 August 2013

EBA prepared a so called discussion paper in November 2012. It presents the EBA's preliminary views. The discussion paper was designed in a way to synthesize all stakeholders' opinions at an early stage and before developing a binding technical standard. Based on the responses, a consultation paper was issued and published in July 2013. This was followed by a draft on the binding technical standard RTS.

This document (dated 2 August 2013) stipulates advice on the treatment of unrealized gains measured at FV.[133]

According to this paper, the *"ability to realise the gains will, however, depend on the nature of the underlying item and the current economic context. For instance, there may be constraints that prevent or limit the ability of an institution to realise the gains such as the lack of an active market or the existence of clauses that restrict the institution's ability to sell (a clause might not allow or impose significant penalties to investors if they want to exit before a specified time)...".*

and

"...Unrealised gains are also subject to movements in the market price. In less liquid markets there is an additional risk that unrealised gains may not be available to absorb losses because the related assets may not be realised in the short term at the price expected by the institution. Thus, realisation of any gains from such investments at any time would be highly uncertain. However, these concerns may be covered by the relevant accounting standards (for instance, IFRS 13) and the upcoming requirements on Prudent Valuation established in Article 105 of the CRR."[134]

"Even if the market is liquid, an institution may not have the intention to realise the unrealised gain In the Discussion paper it was stated that once the public consultation is finalised, the EBA will draft the technical advice that will need to be provided to the Commission by 1 January 2014."[135]

---

[133] EBA, 2013. P.9.
[134] EBA, 2013. P.9.
[135] EBA, 2013. P.1.

However, in addition, an interaction with capital requirements must be considered as a risk of unrealized gains that has already been covered may disappear. This is relevant primarily for the trading book.

In this context, IFRS 13 is also interesting. The article contains the principles to measure illiquid instruments at FV and requires considerations to be made on restrictions to the use of an asset[136] and its specifications. It should therefore be noted that unrealized gains may disappear if the assumptions were wrong.[137]

However, the reliability of fair values and the unrealized gains associated with it is a regulatory concern and could for example be covered by applying an prudential filter on unrealized gains. This would be a necessary amendment to the Prudent Valuation set out in the CRR. Taking these results into consideration, those requirements do not suffice.

4.7 RTS on prudent valuation

4.7.1 Consultation paper on RTS on prudent valuation

EBA prepared a paper in accordance with their mandate provided in the CRR[138].

The consultation paper stipulates the requirement applies to all FV positions. Prudential filters should cover several regulatory concerns as follows:

- Unrealized gains could disappear due to negative impacts to market prices of the underlying items.
- A possible interaction between regulatory capital requirements and the reliability of fair values.

The objective was to assess the reliability of fair values and recommend a prudential filter as a supplement to the prudential valuation methodology. The consultation paper proposes two different approaches to calculating a prudent valuation adjustment:

- The "<u>simplified approach</u>": If the amount of on- and off-balance sheet fair valued assets does not exceed EUR 15 billion. This simplified approach foresees a risk adjustment amounting to 25% of net unrealized profit at FV and 0,1% of the amount of the absolute value of of assets.

---

[136] IFRS, 13.11.
[137] EBA, 2013. P.1.
[138] CRR Article 105.

- A core approach if the amount of on- and off-balance sheet FVA exceeds EUR 15 billion. This approach is more granular and stipulates additional risk adjustments on the fair value.

The paper does not propose any filter for unrealized gains from HfT assets and therefore, no interaction with prudential valuation was considered.

4.7.2 Final RTS

Nearly two years after the CRR came into force, the regulation (EU) 2016/101 was published (on October 26th 2015). It entered into force 20 days after publication. It supplemented the CRR on prudent valuation under Article 105 (14) CRR.

Title and reference

Commission Delegated Regulation (EU) 2016/101 of 26 October 2015 supplementing Regulation (EU) No 575/2013 of the European Parliament and of the Council with regard to regulatory technical standards for prudent valuation under Article 105(14) (Text with EEA relevance)

OJ L 21, 28.1.2016, p. 54–65 (BG, ES, CS, DA, DE, ET, EL, EN, FR, HR, IT, LV, LT, HU, MT, NL, PL, PT, RO, SK, SL, FI, SV)

Chart 10: Publication of RTS on prudent valuation

This standard aims to achieve an *"appropriate degree of certainty having regard to the dynamic nature of trading book positions."* It mostly follows the two approaches described in the consultation paper (the simplified and core approach for fair valued assets and liabilities exceeding EUR 15 billion).

The idea is to estimate the prudent value mark to market. However, if no market data is available, an expert opnion/ estimation can be specified.

Applying the simplified approach, means that an Asset Value Adjustment (AVA) is allocated as described above at the institutional level, while under the alternative approach, an aggregation of single AVAs related to

- "market price uncertainty"
- "model risk"
- "close-out costs"

Has to be done for each category.

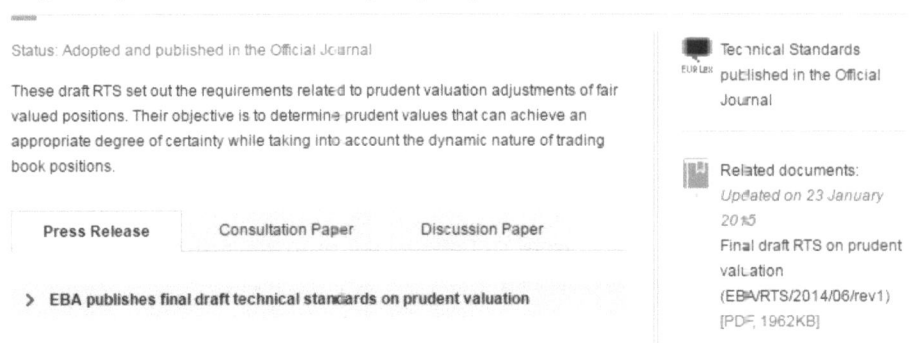

Chart 11: RTS on prudential valuation

It can be concluded that the former prudential filter for AfS positions was not replaced. This filter still partially applies during a transition period only. The RTS on prudential valuation therefore means a significantly weaker regulation in comparison to the pre-crisis CEBS guideline, although AfS positions played such an important role and led to a poor capitalization of banks. The new approach towards prudent valuation is complex, and even if executed in a conservative manner only partially adjusts unrealized gains.

5 CONCLUSION

At the start, this study posed three research questions. In the following section, the insights gained will be applied to answer these questions.

5.1 Question 1: Does the concept of OCI allow capital to leave the bank, although profits have not yet been realized?

The concept of OCI was of upmost importance before, during and in the aftermath of the financial crisis, and it is part of the cause of the financial crisis, though it was not the only cause of the credit crisis. However, the application created a domino effect in a declining economy. This became obvious by IASB's hasty issuance of the amendment to prevent further asset write-offs.

The concept of OCI allows banks to distribute capital although gains have not yet been realized. This is largely the case because unrealized gains increase regulatory capital. Until CRR was implemented, a prudential filter was in place for *"unrealized gains and losses recognized in the revaluation reserve"*.

In case markets become illiquid or market prices deteriorate, the revaluation reserve is immediately affected. This happened incredibly fast in the course of the recent financial crisis. Unrealized gains disappeared and were only partially realized because of bail out programmes like TARP or Quantitative Easening. IFRS has a different scope in this regard and from an accounting perspective, it might be recommendable to park unrealized gains within the revaluation reserve. However, from a prudential perspective, this should raise concern as the concept of OCI allows unrealized gains to leave the bank. In case they cannot be realized, for example, because it turns out there was an asset bubble, the capital base is weakened and in the worst case scenario, this could even lead to a bankruptcy scenario or a need to bail out the bank. If unrealized gains cannot be realized, it becomes obvious that the valuation was too optimistic. This is particularly relevant for IFRS Level 2 and Level 3 assets.

5.2 Question 2: Is the poor capitalization of several banks also a result of IFRS's concept of OCI?

The revaluation reserve did not indicate a sufficient loss absorption capacity during and in the aftermath of the recent financial crisis. This was the main reason for the amendment to IAS 39, which prevented several banks from bankruptcy. The European union itself insisted on this reclassification option and subsequently, the amendment to IAS was issued in 2008. This meant the opportunity for banks to value assets based on amortization costs instead of FV. In addition, the amendment enabled transfers from PnL to OCI.

The unrealized gains could not be realized in market transaction. Therefore, the assumption can only be that pre-crisis valuations were too optimistic and hence not sustainable. The revaluation reserve cannot be considered part of the regulatory capital from a prudential perspective. However, unless a sufficient prudential filter is in place, it is not possible to distribute unrealized gains.

5.3 Question 3: Has the issue been properly addressed by European regulators, particularly in terms of prudential filters?

The Basel III framework does not entail a filter for unrealized gains parked in Other Comprehensive Income as was the case before the CRR. The RTS on prudential valuation, which entered into force two years after CRR, implies a loosening of regulations in this regard.

Taking into account that this issue is one of the main reasons for the poor capitalization of several banks, which were hit hard by the financial crisis, this is not reasonable and therefore has not been properly addressed so far.

Taking into consideration that a lot of new regulations and regulatory bodies were introduced with Basel III, it seems that the root cause has not been sufficiently addressed by regulators.

This tesis clearly demonstrates that there are a number of good arguments to implement an additional prudential filter on unrealized gains. Most importantly, unrealized gains may not be fully available to cover future losses.

However, it must be pointed out that the scope of this book focused primarily on Other Comprehensive Income. Therefore, it does not take possible capital requirements or prudential filters for all fair value positions into account.

Regulators are aware of the problem and even received a mandate to address it through Article 105 CRR, but their mandate was not used to maintain the *"Prudential filter for unrealized gains and losses recognized in the revaluation reserve"* which existed before the CRR came into force.

There is only one option to adequately address regulatory concerns in a sustainable way and this is the implementation of a prudential filter. Unrealized gains shall not be considered in regulatory cpital. This represents the most prudent option as it entails the exclusion of unrealized gains in regulatory capital.[139]

The CRR is a clear step back in comparison to pre-crisis regulations on this topic. At present, CRR entails the inclusion of unrealized gains without any adjustment in CET1.

EBA should consider alternatives for a feasible prudential filter.[140] The recently adopted RTS on prudential valuation significantly weakens the regulation in this regard and appears to be insufficient based on the findings of this book. The IASB plans to replace this standard with IFRS 9. However, IFRS 9 has already been discussed for years but has yet to be implemented.

---

[139] EBA, 2013, Discussion Paper. P.9.
[140] EBA, 2013, Discussion Paper. P.9.

BIBLIOGRAPHY

Agrimon, I./ Dietsch, M./ Estrada, A. (2015): (PRUDENTIAL FILTERS, PORTFOLIO COMPOSITION AND CAPITAL RATIOS IN EUROPEAN BANKS), SBIF 90TH ANNIVERSARY CONFERENCE, Santiago de Chile
Allen, F. /Carletti, E. 2008: (Mark-to-market accounting and liquidity pricing) in. Journal of Economics and Accounting, no. 45, 358-375
Audit Committee Institute (2012): (Insights into IFRS: an overview), London, UK
Banque de France (2008): (Financial stability review, Special issue on valuation), Paris, France
Barth, M. (1994): (Fair value accounting: Evidence from investment securities and the market valuation of banks) in: European Accounting Review
Barth, M. (2006): (Including estimates of the future in today's financial statements) Accounting Horizons, 20, 271-286
Barth, M./ Landsman (2010): (How did Financial Reporting Contribute to the Financial Crisis), European Accounting Review
Barth, M. et all (2014), (Bank Earnings and Regulatory Capital Management Using Available for Sale Securities), Accounting Horizons, 20, 271-286
Bianco, T. (2009): (Gli strumenti finanziari. Strumenti finanziari - 2 Agenda Strumenti finanziari Iscrizione iniziale e valutazione successiva Impairment Derecognitio) XXXIV CONGRESSO NAZIONALE ANDAF, Venice, Italy
BIS Bank for International Settlements (2010): Basel Committee on Banking Supervision: (Basel III: A global regulatory framework for more resilient banks and banking systems) URL: http://www.bis.org/publ/bcbs189.pdf, 23.01.2016, Basel, Switzerland
BIS Bank for International Settlements (2016): Basel Committee on Banking Supervision: (Working Paper No 30 Literature review on integration of regulatory capital and liquidity instruments), Basel, Switzerland
BIS Bank for International Settlements: Basel Committee on Banking Supervision (2010): (Basel III: A global regulatory framework for more resilient banks and banking systems), December 2010 (rev June 2011), Basel, Switzerland
BIS Bank for International Settlements: Basel Committee on Banking Supervision (2015): (Accounting Task Force of the Basel Committee), Basel, Switzerland
BIS Bank for International Settlements: Basel Committee on Banking Supervision (2015): (Working Paper 28 - The interplay of accounting and regulation and its impact on bank behavior), Basel, Switzerland
BIS Bank for International Settlements: Shin Song Hyong - Bank capital and monetary policy transmission (2016): Panel remarks at the ECB and its Watchers XVII conference; Frankfurt, Germany
Bischof, J. /Brüggemann, U./ Daske, H. (2012): (SFB 649 Discussion Paper 2012-010 Fair Value Reclassifications of Financial Assets during the Financial Crisis), Mannheim, Germany
Bischof, J. Brüggemann, U. (2010): (Relaxation of Fair Value Rules in Times of Crisis), An Analysis of Economic Benefits and Costs of the Amendment to IAS 39), Mannheim, Germany
Bischof, J./ Daske, H. (2011): (Fair Value Accounting and the Business Model of Banks), Mannheim, Germany
Braunberger, G. (2016): (Banken schütten zu viel Geld aus), Frankfurt. 29.04.2016. In: Frankfurter Allgemeine Zeitung, URL: http://www.faz.net/-gv6-8ggv8 Banken schütten zu viel Geld aus, Frankfurt, Germany

Brüggemann, J./ Daske, H. (2012): (Fair Value Reclassifications of Financial Assets during the Financial Crisis), Mannheim, Germany

Casabona, P./ Shoaf, V. (2010): (Fair Value Accounting and the Credit Crisis), Research Papers, The Peter J. Tobin College of Business, St. John's University, New York, USA

CEBS Guideline on prudential valuation (2004): (Guidelines on Prudential Filters for Regulatory Capital), London, UK

CFA Institute: (Financial Crisis Insights on Bank Performance Reporting)

CRR Regulation (EU) 575/2013 (Capital Requirements Regulation - CRR), 2016/04/15

Database „Bankscope" (Bankscope is a global database of banks financial statements,) URL: http://www.bvdinfo.com/en-gb/our-products/company-information/international-roducts/bankscope, 2016 February 22nd

De La Dehesa, G. (2009): (La primera gran crisis financiera del siglo XXI. Orígenes, detonantes, efectos, respuestas y remedies). Alianza Editorial

Deutsche Bank AG: (Financial Statement, 2012), Frankfurt, Germany

Deutsche Bundesbank, Zentralbereich Banken und Finanzaufsicht (2011): (Basel III – Leitfaden), Frankfurt, Germany

Doralt, W. (2014): (Kodex des internationalen Rechts: IAS/ IFRS Internationale Rechnungslegung), Vienna, Austria,

EBA (2013): (Consultation Paper Draft Regulatory Technical Standards (RTS) On prudent valuation under Article 105(14) of Regulation (EU) 575/2013 (Capital Requirements Regulation - CRR), EBA CP/2013/28, London, UK

EBA (2013): (Discussion Paper: Technical Advice to the Commission on possible treatments of unrealised gains measured at fair value under Article 80 of the Capital Requirements Regulation CRR), London, UK

EBA (2014): (EBA_CP_2013_28_Prudent Valuation EBA-DP-2013-03 (DP Technical Advice unrealised gains), EBA_CP_2013_28_Prudent Valuation EBA-DP-2013-03. London, UK

EBA (2015): (FINAL draft Regulatory Technical Standards on prudent valuation under Article 105(14) of Regulation (EU) No 575/2013 (Capital Requirements Regulation — CRR), London, UK

EBF European Banking Federation (2013): (Comments on the Discussion papers on technical advice on possible treatments of unrealized gains measured at fair value), EBA DP 2013/03), URL: http://www.ebf-fbe.eu/uploads/EBF_004470 - Final EBF Comments on EBA-DP-2013-03 (Unrealised Gains).pdf, 13.01.2016, Brussels, Belgium

ECB (2016): (Panel remarks at The ECB and its Watchers XVII conference Frankfurt, 7 April 2016) Frankfurt, Germany

Ernstberger, J. (2010): (Reclassification of Financial Instruments in the Financial Crisis –Evidence from the European Banking Sector), Bochum, Germany

European Banking Authority EBA (2004): (CEBS/04/91 21 December 2004 GUIDELINES ON PRUDENTIAL FILTERS FOR REGULATORY CAPITAL), URL:http://www.eba.europa.eu/documents/10180/16094/prudential_filters 21 Dec 2004.pdf, 12.12.2015, London, UK

European Banking Authority EBA (2013): (Discussion Paper 17), London, UK

European Banking Authority EBA (2013): (Technical Advice to the Commission on possible treatments of unrealised gains measured at fair value under Article 80 of the Capital Requirements Regulation (CRR), EBA/DP/2013/03, 2 August 2013, London, UK

European Central Bank ECB (2004): (Financial Stability Review), Frankfurt, Germany

European Central Bank ECB (2005,2007,2009,2015): (Financial Stability Review), Frankfurt, Germany

European Commission (2008): (Regulation 1004/2008 as of October 15, 2008), in: Amtsblatt der Europäischen Union, L275/37
European Commission (2014): (Economic Review of the Financial Regulation Agenda), COMMISSION STAFF WORKING DOCUMENT, Brussels, Belgium
European Union (EU), (2008): (Press release October 7th 2008)
Farkas-Novotny, Z., Fiechter, P. (2011): (Pricing of Fair Values during the Financial Crisis: International Evidence), Working paper, Frankfurt, Germany
Fernandez, F. S. (2010): (Effects Of Comprehensive Income On RCE In A Context Of Crisis: Empirical Evidence For IBEX-35 Listed Companies (2004-2008)), in: International Business & Economics Research Journal – January 2010 Volume 9, Number 1 117, Cantabria, Spain
Fiechter, P. (2011): (Reclassification of Financial Assets under IAS 39: Impact on European Banks' Financial Statements), Zurich, Switzerland
Financial Accounting Standards Board (FASB) (2009): (The Fair Value Option for Financial Assets and Financial Liabilities, Including an Amendment of FASB Statement No. 115, Elements, par. 70), Accounting Horizons, 21 (2), 189-200
Financial Stability Forum (FSF) (2008): (Recommendations of the Financial Stability Forum), Proposed amendments to IAS 39 and IFRS 7, international committee
Forbes, S. (2009). :(End Mark-to-Market) Internet: www.forbes.com, 12.03.2016
Gabler Wirtschaftslexikon (2016): (URL: http://wirtschaftslexikon.gabler.de/Archiv/4361496/prudential-filter-v5.html). Aufruf 12.04.2016
Gambacorta, L. / Shin,H.S.: "Why bank capital matters for monetary policy", BIS Working Papers, no 558, April 2016, Basel, Switzerland
Gazzolaa, P./ Ameliob, S. (2014): (The impact of comprehensive income on the financial ratios)
Gingrich, N. (2008): (Suspend mark-to-market now!) Forbes, 29.09.2008.
Glavan, S. (2010): (Fair value accounting in banks and the recent financial crisis) Estabilidad financier (19), 55-69
Guest, R. (2011): (The Global Financial Crisis and Undergraduate Macroeconomics). In: Australian Economic Review, 44(1), pp. 113–120.
Hall, R. (2010): (Why Does the Economy Fall to Pieces after a Financial Crisis?). In: Journal of Economic Perspectives, no. 24, 3–20
Hirst, E./ Hopkins, P. (1998): (Comprehensive income reporting and analysts valuation judgments.) in: Journal of Accounting Research, no. 36, 47–75
Hitz, J.-M. (2007): (The Decision Usefulness of Fair Value Accounting – A Theoretical Perspective) in: European Accounting Review, no. 16 , 323-362
Hoogervorst (2014): (The Dangers of Ignoring Unrealised Income), European Commission
IAS (2016): (URL: www.iasplus.com/en/images/old/publications/united-states/heads-up/vol-21-issue-20-1). 16.03.2016
International Accounting Standard Board IASB (2008): (Amendment to IAS 39 Reclassification of Financial Assets)
Jarolim, N., Öppinher, C. (2012): (Fair Value Accounting in Times of FinanciL Crisis), in: ACRN Journal of Finance and Risk Perspectives Vol. 1, Issue 1, p. 67-90
Kholmy, K./ Ernstberger, J. (2012): (Reclassification of Financial Instruments in the Financial Crisis – Evidence from the European Banking Sector), in: (Fair Value Accounting for Financial Instruments and Analysts' Forecasts in the Financial Crisis), Bochum, Germany
Kholmy, K. (2012): (Fair Value Accounting for Financial Instruments and Analysts' Forecasts in the Financial Crisis), Dissertatitionsschrift, Ruhr-Universität Bochum, Bochum, Germany
Kilicer, Y. (2010): (Fair-Value Bilanzierung in der Finanzkrise), Hamburg, Germany

KPMG (2008): (Flash Report: Reclassification Amendment to IAS 39 Financial Instruments, recognition and Measurement), Berlin, Germany

Laux, C./ Leuz, C. (2009): (The crisis of fair value accounting: Making sense of the recent debate). Accounting organization and society 34, 826-834. Luax, Christian; Leuz, Christian (2009): The Crisis of Fair Value Accounting: URL: http://papers.ssrn.com/sol3/papers.cfm?abstract_id=1392645 vom 10.11.2009.

Laux, C. Leuz, C. (2010): (Forthcoming in the Journal of Economic Perspectives 2010), Frankfurt, Germany

Magnan, M.L. (2009): (Fair Value Accounting and the Financial Crisis: Messenger or Contributor?), AP Vol. 8 No. 3 — PC vol. 8, no 3, pages 189 – 213

Paanen, M. / Renders, A. / Shima, K. (2012): (The Amendment of IAS 39 Determinants of Reclassification Behavior and Capital Market Consequences), In: Journal of Accounting, Auditing and Finance, vol. 27 no. 2 208-235, Maastricht, Netherlands, East Bay, USA

Papa, V. (2013): (European Bank Reporting: Investors Should be Wary of Reclassified Financial Assets), CFA Institute Market Integrity Insights Views on the integrity of global capital markets, CFA Institute URL: https://blogs.cfainstitute.org/marketintegrity/2013/05/01/european-bank-reporting-investors-should-be-wary-of-reclassified-financial-assets, 23.01.2016

Platin, G. /Sapra H./ Shin (2008a): (Marking-to-Market: Panacea or Pandora's Box), Journal of Accounting Research, 46, 435-460

Platin, G. /Sapra H./ Shin (2008b): (Fair value accounting and financial stability), Financial Stability Review, 12, 85-94

Russo, T.A., Katzel, A.J. (2011): (The 2008 Financial Crisis and Its Aftermath: Adressing the next Debt Challenge), Occassional Paper 82, Group of Thirty, Washington, USA

Ryan, S. (2008): (Accounting in and for the Subprime Crisis) in: The Accounting Review, no. 83, 1605-1638

Sanders, S. (2010): (Fair Value Accounting: Villain or Innocent Victim Exploring the Links between Fair Value Accounting, Bank Regulatory Capital and the Recent Financial Crisis), Federal Reserve Bank of Boston, USA

Schipper, K. (2005): (The Introduction of International Accounting Standards in Europe: Implications for International Convergence) In: European Accounting Review, no. 14

Securities and Exchange Commission (SEC) (2007): (Public Comment on Role of IFRS in the U.S)

Securities and Exchange Commission (SEC) (2008): (Report and Recommendations Pursuant to Section 133 of the Emergency Economic Stabilization Act of 2008: Study on Mark-to-Market Accounting)

SFAS (2010): (Statement of Financial Accounting Standards – SFAS – No. 130 Reporting Comprehensive Income)

Shin, H.S. BIS (2016): (Bank capital and monetary policy transmission), Hyun Song Shin1 Economic Adviser and Head of Research, BIS, (URL: https://www.bis.org/speeches/sp160407.pdf), URL: http://www.bis.org/speeches/sp160407.pdf, 22.04.2016, Basel, Switzerland

Stegmann, C. / Klauck, K.O. (2012): (Basel III: Vom regulatorischen Rahmen zu einer risikoadäquaten Gesamtbanksteuerung), Frankfurt, Germany

Orrick (2011) publication: (URL: https://www.orrick.com/Events-and-Publications/Documents/1782.pdf), 03.03.2016, New York, USA

Tarapada Ghosh (2013): (IFRS accounting for financial assets and financial liabilities), Dubai

U.S. Congress (2008): (URL: US congress http://www.iasplus.com/en/images/old/publications/united-states/heads-up/vol-21-issue-20-1), USA, 15.05.2016

Wallison, P. J. (2008): (Fair Value Accounting: A Critique), American Enterprise Institute for Public Policy Research Outlook Series, USA
Wallison, P. J. (2008): (Judgment too Important to be left to the Accountants), in: Financial Times, New York, USA
Wallison, P.J. (2015): (Hidden in Plain Sight), Encounter Books, Washington, USA
Whalen, R. C. (2008): (The Subprime Crisis – Cause, Effect and Consequences), Networks Financial Institute, USA
Wilch, A. 2015: UniCredit Group: (impact-of-ssm-and-srep-on-bank-steering-in-a-large-european-banking-group), URL: (http://www.slideshare.net/Lszlrvai/impact-of-ssm-and-srep-on-bank-steering-in-a-large-european-banking-group, München, Germany. Aufruf am 12.04.2016
Wiley insights IFRS: (Interpretation and Application of International Financial Reporting Standards)
Yifan Zhan (2013): (The effect of reclassification under amendment to IAS 39 on liquidity of bank stocks in the EU), Tilburg, Germany
Zandi, M.: (2008): (Chief Economist, Moody's Economy.com) Knight Ridder, September 28, 2008
Zion, D./ Varshney/ Cornett (2009) (Focusing on fair value), Credit Suisse Equity Research, Zürich, Switzerland